SUMMARY OF THE ASCENSION DIMENSION

Exercising Kingdom Authority to Triumph over Circumstances and Opposition

ISAAC PITRE

D DESTINY IMAGE

Destiny Image P.O. Box 310, Shippensburg, PA 17257-0310

This book and all other Destiny Image's books are available at Christian bookstores and distributors worldwide.

For Worldwide Distribution.

Reach us on the Internet: www.destinyimage.com.

ISBN 13 TP: 9798881504403

ISBN 13 eBook: 9798881504410

CONTENTS

INTRODUCTION

Welcome to the "Summary of Ascension Dimension," a transformative exploration of the spiritual elevation that believers are called to experience through Christ's resurrection and ascension. This book seeks to unpack the profound truths and powerful implications of living in the realm of the Ascension Dimension—an existence where heavenly places are not a distant reality but an accessible domain where we are seated with Christ, far above all earthly limitations.

The Ascension Dimension is not merely a theological concept but a practical reality that impacts every aspect of a believer's life. From the way we pray and worship to how we conduct our daily interactions, the understanding that we are raised with Christ changes everything. This summary aims to bring clarity and actionable insights into how to actively engage with this heavenly reality, empowering readers to live a life marked by spiritual authority and divine presence.

Each chapter of this summary distills key themes from comprehensive discussions on the roles of the Holy Spirit, the power of prayer, and the authority endowed to us as co-heirs with Christ. Readers will find themselves invited into a deeper relationship with God, where the barriers between the spiritual and the temporal are blurred, thanks to the indwelling of the Holy Spirit.

As you embark on this journey through the "Summary of Ascension Dimension," expect to encounter a series of transformative truths that will challenge you to rethink your spiritual posture and encourage you to operate from your rightful place in the heavenly realms. This is not just about understanding your spiritual position but actively engaging with it to affect change in your life and the world around you.

Through biblical insights, contemporary applications, and heartfelt prayer, this book will guide you to not only understand but also practice the reality of living in the Ascension Dimension. Prepare to expand your spiritual horizons and embrace your divine destiny as you step into the fullness of what it means to live ascended.

CHAPTER 1

THE REST OF THE STORY PHASE

Bible Verse

Ephesians 2:6 (KJV) - "And hath raised us up together, and made us sit together in heavenly places in Christ Jesus."

Introduction

This chapter delves into the often-overlooked aspect of Jesus' redemptive work—the Ascension—and its significance in the life of a believer. It argues that while the death, burial, and resurrection of Christ are foundational to Christian faith, the fullness of the gospel includes His ascension, where He is seated at the right hand of the Father, completing the work of redemption.

Word of Wisdom

"Take Back Your Authority, the born-

again experience is literally a raising of your spirit from the dead." Isaac Pitre

Main Theme

The chapter emphasizes the Ascension of Jesus as the consummation of His work on earth, which not only completed the stages of redemption but also provided believers with a spiritual position of authority alongside Christ in the heavenly realms.

Key Points

- Jesus' Ascension is crucial as it marks the completion of His redemptive work.
- Believers are spiritually seated with Christ in the heavenly realms, sharing in His authority.
- The Ascension enables believers to live in victory over sin and death.
- Understanding our heavenly seating helps realize the full scope of Christian spiritual authority.
- The Ascension is not just a historical event but a present reality impacting believers.
- This theological insight is essential for a full grasp of the gospel and its implications for daily living.

Key Themes

- **Spiritual Unity with Christ:** Through the Ascension, believers are not only forgiven but are also granted a position of power and authority. This unity with Christ in His resurrection and ascension transforms how they should view themselves and their spiritual capabilities.
- **The Completeness of Redemption:** The Ascension of Jesus is critical for understanding the completeness of redemption. It goes beyond the cross and the grave to include a glorious enthronement that believers partake in, which is essential for living a victorious Christian life.
- **Theological Depth and Practical Implications:** The doctrine of Ascension adds depth to our theological understanding and has practical implications for Christian living, emphasizing victory over spiritual death and a life lived in the authority of Christ.
- **Eternal Perspective in Christian Faith:** Recognizing that Jesus is seated at the right hand of the Father encourages believers to look beyond the temporal and understand their eternal position and calling in Christ.
- **Empowerment through Spiritual Realization:** Understanding our position with Christ in the heavenly realms empowers believers to exercise their God-given authority, impacting how they

Conclusion

The Ascension of Jesus is a fundamental yet often neglected aspect of the gospel that provides a more complete understanding of Christ's work and our role in it. By realizing and embracing our position seated with Christ in heavenly places, believers can walk in the fullness of authority and victory that this truth offers. This chapter urges readers to shift their perspective upward, recognizing that while the grave is empty, the throne is gloriously occupied.

CHAPTER 2

THE DEVIL NEVER SAW IT COMING

Bible Verse

Ephesians 1:20-21 (KJV) - "Which he wrought in Christ, when he raised him from the dead, and set him at his own right hand in the heavenly places, Far above all principality, and power, and might, and dominion, and every name that is named, not only in this world, but also in that which is to come."

Introduction

This chapter reveals the profound mystery of Christ's resurrection and ascension, emphasizing how these events were concealed from both human understanding and demonic powers until revealed through the apostle Paul. It highlights Paul's unique role in disclosing the full scope of the gospel, including the believer's elevated position with Christ.

Word of Wisdom

"Paul was relating to the Church, that the things they couldn't see and hear have now been revealed." Isaac Pitre

Main Theme

Exploring the secretive yet monumental nature of Christ's ascension and the believer's joint seating in heavenly places, this chapter unfolds the unexpected and strategic elements of God's redemption plan which were hidden from all until revealed to Paul.

Key Points

- Paul received the full revelation of Christ's work directly from Jesus, not from human teachings.
- His revelation included the unknown aspects of Christ's resurrection and ascension.
- This divine revelation was kept secret from Satan, who unwittingly played into God's plan.
- Believers share in Jesus' authority and victory through their spiritual union with Him.
- Paul's mission was to enlighten the church about their empowered spiritual position.

- The ultimate purpose of this revelation is for the Church to enforce and demonstrate God's wisdom to the spiritual realms.

Key Themes

- **Paul's Unique Apostolic Role:** Paul's transformation from persecutor to apostle uniquely positioned him to receive and impart the hidden wisdom of God concerning Christ's work. His teachings are foundational for understanding our authority as believers and the spiritual dynamics at play.
- **Strategic Secrecy of Redemption:** The secrecy surrounding Christ's resurrection and ascension served a divine purpose, ensuring the fulfillment of God's plan without interference from demonic powers. This strategic concealment underscores the complexity and power of God's plans.
- **Empowerment through Revelation:** The revelation given to Paul and shared with the Church is not merely doctrinal but empowers believers to live out their heavenly mandate. Knowing we are seated with Christ changes how we view our authority and engage in spiritual warfare.
- **Church's Authority Over Spiritual Realms:** The Church is called to manifest and teach the profound truths of Christ's victory to principalities and powers. This task underscores the Church's role in

God's plan, extending beyond personal salvation to cosmic revelation.

- **Continuity of the Apostolic Mission:** Paul's prayers for the Ephesians to comprehend their spiritual stature continue to be relevant. The Church is tasked with not only understanding but actively demonstrating the power and authority vested in us through Christ's ascension.

Conclusion

Paul's revelations about the resurrection and ascension of Christ reveal a hidden dimension of God's redemption plan, positioning the Church in a place of unprecedented spiritual authority. This chapter challenges believers to embrace and walk in this authority, ensuring that the fullness of Christ's victory is known and manifested on Earth as it is in Heaven. The implications of this truth are vast, not just for individual believers but for the entire Church as it confronts spiritual dominions with the reality of Christ's triumph.

CHAPTER 3

THE ASCENDED CHURCH

Bible Verse

Ephesians 1:22-23 (KJV) - "And hath put all things under his feet, and gave him to be the head over all things to the church, Which is his body, the fulness of him that filleth all in all."

Introduction

This chapter discusses the profound implications of Jesus' ascension for the Church, emphasizing how this event extends the authority of Christ to His followers in both the spiritual and earthly realms. It explores the strategic victory over Satan through Christ's ascension and how this positions the Church in a place of power.

Word of Wisdom

"The purpose for the church was to be the body, or governing entity, to en-

force Jesus's authority in the heavenly places!" Isaac Pitre

Main Theme

The chapter elaborates on the significant shift in spiritual authority from Satan to the Church through Christ's ascension, explaining how this transition affects the believer's role and responsibility in the Kingdom of God.

Key Points

- The ascension of Jesus Christ marked a pivotal victory over the powers of darkness.
- This event signified the transfer of authority from Satan to Christ, and subsequently to the Church.
- Believers are not just saved; they are called to enforce Jesus' victory over spiritual darkness.
- The Church's authority extends into both the spiritual and the natural realms.
- Understanding our heavenly seating is crucial for executing our kingdom mandate.
- The Spirit of God reveals the deep implications of our spiritual authority to us.

Key Themes

- **Dual Realms of Authority:** The ascension of Jesus establishes the Church's authority in both the spiritual and earthly realms, empowering believers to operate beyond natural limitations. This dual authority enables the Church to enforce the victory of Christ over demonic powers and to extend the Kingdom of God effectively on earth.

- **Strategic Importance of Ascension:** The ascension is not merely a historical event but a strategic victory that shifted the balance of spiritual power. It marks the fulfillment of God's promise to ruin Satan's plans and establish His own authority through Christ and His Church.

- **Role of the Holy Spirit in Revelation:** The Holy Spirit plays a crucial role in revealing the truths of spiritual authority to the Church. Without the Spirit's revelation, the profound realities of our position with Christ in the heavenly realms remain obscured and underutilized.

- **Implications for Spiritual Warfare:** Understanding our position in Christ equips the Church to engage effectively in spiritual warfare. The authority delegated to us through Christ's ascension is meant to be actively exercised in confronting and dismantling the works of darkness.

- **Church's Governance in Spiritual Realities:** The Church is called to govern as Christ's body, making known the manifold wisdom of God to principalities and powers. This governance is not just over earthly matters but encompasses the broader spiritual duties assigned to the Church.

Conclusion

The ascension of Jesus Christ is central to understanding the Church's role and authority in the spiritual realm. As believers grasp the full extent of what it means to be seated with Christ in heavenly places, they are called to move beyond mere acknowledgment to active engagement in enforcing the victory Christ secured. This chapter challenges believers to embrace their delegated authority and fulfill their divine mandate as representatives of Christ's kingdom, both in the spiritual and natural realms.

CHAPTER 4

FILLING THE HEAVENS

Bible Verse

Ephesians 6:12 (KJV) - "For we wrestle not against flesh and blood, but against principalities, against powers, against the rulers of the darkness of this world, against spiritual wickedness in high places."

Introduction

This chapter explores the strategic victory of Jesus' ascension and its implications for the Church's authority over spiritual realms. It delves into the concept that the Church is not only saved from sin but is also empowered to enforce Jesus' triumph over satanic forces.

Word of Wisdom

"If the whole body of Christ would assemble in the heavens, and exercise

Jesus's authority, we could see nations shaken in a day." Isaac Pitre

Main Theme

The chapter discusses the transfer of authority from Satan to the Church through Christ's ascension, emphasizing the believer's role in continuing Jesus' ministry of disrupting the works of darkness and enforcing the Kingdom of God on earth and in the heavenly realms.

Key Points

- Jesus' ascension stripped Satan of unchecked authority in both the earthly and spiritual realms.
- The authority over earth originally given to Adam, which was usurped by Satan, has been reclaimed by Christ.
- Believers are called to enforce Jesus' authority over demonic forces.
- The Church is to fill the heavens, leaving no place for Satan to operate freely.
- Spiritual warfare is not about defeating Satan—a victory already won by Christ— but about enforcing that victory.
- The Church's role extends beyond earthly gatherings, requiring spiritual assembly and action in heavenly places.

Key Themes

- **Authority Transfer and Its Enforcement:** Through Christ's ascension, all authority in heaven and on earth was reclaimed and is now shared with the Church. Believers are empowered to enforce this authority in the spiritual realm, affecting changes on earth by restricting demonic activities and influences.

- **Strategic Spiritual Warfare:** The battle against spiritual forces is not just defensive but offensive, requiring believers to actively displace demonic influences from their territories. This warfare is crucial for the manifestation of God's kingdom on earth as it is in heaven.

- **Role of the Holy Spirit in Revealing Authority:** Understanding the full scope of our authority in Christ is revealed through the Holy Spirit. This revelation is essential for believers to effectively engage in spiritual warfare and enforce the victory already won by Christ.

- **Impact of Unified Spiritual Assembly:** The collective action of the Church in the heavenly realms is vital. When believers unite in their spiritual authority, significant transformations in societal, cultural, and global dimensions are possible.

- **Continuous Enforcement Until Christ's Return:** The Church's mandate to enforce Christ's authority will continue until all things are subjected under His feet at His return. This ongoing task underscores the Church's proactive role in spiritual governance and territorial dominion.

Conclusion

The ascension of Jesus is a call to arms for the Church, positioning believers in a place of immense spiritual authority and responsibility. This chapter compels the Church to rise to its full stature as the enforcer of Heaven's rule on earth, challenging believers to live out their heavenly mandate with authority and urgency. By doing so, the Church not only honors Christ's victory but actively participates in the kingdom's advancement against all opposing forces.

CHAPTER 5

HEAVEN AND HEAVENLY PLACES

Bible Verse

Ephesians 1:13-14 (KJV) - "In whom ye also trusted, after that ye heard the word of truth, the gospel of your salvation: in whom also after that ye believed, ye were sealed with that Holy Spirit of promise, Which is the earnest of our inheritance until the redemption of the purchased possession, unto the praise of his glory."

Introduction

This chapter distinguishes between the concepts of "Heaven" and "heavenly places" as described in the Bible, clarifying the believer's current and future positions in relation to Christ's authority and the spiritual realm.

Word of Wisdom

"The Spirit has been given to us to

manifest the down payment of Heaven on earth!" Isaac Pitre

Main Theme

The chapter explains the dual realities of a Christian's life: the present, active engagement in spiritual battles utilizing Christ's authority in heavenly places, and the future, eternal rest in Heaven devoid of conflict.

Key Points

- Heavenly places refer to a current spiritual reality where believers can exercise Christ's authority.
- Heaven is a future physical reality where believers will experience eternal rest and glory.
- Believers are sealed with the Holy Spirit as a down payment of our future inheritance.
- The Holy Spirit's role includes empowering believers to manifest heavenly realities on earth.
- The promises of God include both current benefits and future fulfillment in Heaven.
- Redemption is experienced in two parts: now on Earth through the Spirit, and fully in Heaven.

Key Themes

- **Current vs. Future Inheritance:** While Heaven is the final, unblemished reality awaiting believers, heavenly places represent the current spiritual battlefield where believers exercise Christ's authority against dark powers. This dual focus requires understanding and active participation in spiritual warfare as well as hope for future rest.

- **Role of the Holy Spirit:** The Holy Spirit's sealing of believers is both a mark of God's ownership and a deposit guaranteeing our heavenly inheritance. This sealing empowers believers to live victoriously over sin and Satan by manifesting aspects of heavenly life here on earth.

- **Spiritual Authority and Warfare:** Believers are called to enforce Jesus' victory over Satan by actively engaging in spiritual warfare. This authority is not just for future enjoyment but for current application in overcoming evil and advancing God's kingdom on Earth.

- **Redemptive Reality on Earth:** The redemption promised to believers is partially experienced now through healing, deliverance, and spiritual victory. These are foretastes of the full redemption and glorification awaiting in Heaven, demonstrating the already-but-not-yet nature of our salvation.

- **Promises as Foretastes of Heaven:** The promises of God serve as glimpses of what will be fully realized in Heaven but can be partly enjoyed now. Each promise fulfilled on Earth by the Spirit's power is a testament to the eventual complete fulfillment in the eternal state.

Conclusion

The ascension of Christ has significant implications for believers, both in their current spiritual engagements and their future eternal state. Understanding the distinction between "Heaven" and "heavenly places" allows believers to more effectively live out their faith, wielding the authority given to them to overcome spiritual adversaries and manifest aspects of heavenly life on Earth, all while looking forward to the complete fulfillment of God's promises in Heaven. This chapter calls believers to a deeper realization of their present role and future hope, urging them to actively partake in Christ's victory and authority.

CHAPTER 6

CROWNED BY GRACE

Bible Verse

Hebrews 1:3-4 (KJV) - "Who being the brightness of his glory, and the express image of his person, and upholding all things by the word of his power, when he had by himself purged our sins, sat down on the right hand of the Majesty on high; Being made so much better than the angels, as he hath by inheritance obtained a more excellent name than they."

Introduction

This chapter explores the significance of Jesus' position at the right hand of the Father, emphasizing not only the authority but also the majesty that comes with this seat. It reflects on how believers, too, are invited to share in this royal status through grace, transforming their identity and purpose.

Word of Wisdom

"We are not in this position because of anything we've done! You're in this position because of what Jesus has done!"
Isaac Pitre

Main Theme

The concept of grace not only as a means of salvation but as a crowning of believers with majesty, authority, and a new identity in Christ. The chapter details how this transformation impacts the believer's life and their spiritual warfare.

Key Points

- Jesus' seating at the right hand of the Father represents supreme authority and majesty.
- Believers share in this royal status through the grace given by Christ.
- Our identity shifts from sinners to royal heirs when we accept Christ's sacrifice and ascension.
- Spiritual warfare and authority stem from this new position of power over principalities and darkness.
- The Holy Spirit seals believers as a down payment, affirming our inheritance both now and in the future.

- The majesty of Christ is meant to be reflected in the lives of believers as they execute their royal duties on Earth.

Key Themes

- **Transformation Through Grace:** The grace bestowed upon believers is not just for salvation but also for elevating them to a position of royal authority alongside Christ. This shift in identity from sinners to sons and daughters of God involves a deep transformation, affecting how believers see themselves and their purpose on Earth.
- **Majesty in Authority:** Sitting at the right hand of the Father is a symbol of ultimate authority and majesty. This position is one of active reign, where Jesus, and by extension, His followers, execute dominion over spiritual realms, bringing about God's will on Earth as it is in Heaven.
- **The Role of the Holy Spirit:** The Holy Spirit's role as the seal and guarantee of our inheritance is crucial for understanding and accessing the benefits of our royal status now. The Spirit empowers believers to live out their heavenly mandate even while on Earth.
- **Implications for Spiritual Warfare:** Understanding our royal authority and majesty through Christ changes the approach and effectiveness of spiritual

warfare. Believers are called to enforce Christ's victory over the devil, not from a position of striving but from one of assured victory and authority.

- **Identity and Inheritance:** The majesty we are crowned with by grace should redefine our self-perception and our interactions with the world. This new identity carries responsibilities—to live as kings and priests who rightly represent the Kingdom of God, administering justice, mercy, and grace.

Conclusion

The majesty and authority granted to believers through Christ's ascension and seating at the right hand of the Father are transformative. This chapter calls believers to embrace their royal identity, understand the depth of their inheritance in Christ, and live out their divine purpose with the authority that has been graciously bestowed upon them. By doing so, believers can effectively bring about God's kingdom on Earth, reflecting the majesty of Christ in their daily lives.

CHAPTER 7

SPIRITUAL BLESSINGS

Bible Verse

Ephesians 1:3 (KJV) - "Blessed be the God and Father of our Lord Jesus Christ, who hath blessed us with all spiritual blessings in heavenly places in Christ."

Introduction

This chapter emphasizes the importance of spiritual blessings that believers receive in Christ, which empower and authorize them to operate effectively in the spiritual realm. It contrasts spiritual blessings with material blessings, underscoring their eternal value and immediate applicability in the believer's life.

Word of Wisdom

"We are heirs and joint heirs with Christ. Jesus is greatly honored when we claim what's ours." Isaac Pitre

Main Theme

The chapter discusses the various spiritual blessings that are accessible to believers through Christ's ascension, explaining how these blessings not only benefit believers spiritually but also have practical implications for their earthly lives.

Key Points

• Spiritual blessings are given to believers to empower their spiritual life and authority.

• These blessings are part of our inheritance through Christ and are accessible now.

• Believers are authorized to function in the spiritual dimension with the privileges of Jesus.

• Spiritual blessings include redemption, wisdom, and an identity shift from sinners to royal heirs.

• Understanding and accessing these blessings require recognition of our spiritual position in Christ.

• Spiritual blessings are meant to be actively claimed and utilized, not passively awaited.

Key Themes

• **Nature and Purpose of Spiritual Blessings:** Spiritual blessings are designed to equip believers to manifest God's kingdom on Earth as it is in Heaven. These blessings authorize believers to live in victory over spiritual darkness and to influence the physical world through spiritual means.

- **Accessibility and Immediate Application:** The blessings that come from being in Christ are not just future promises but present realities. Believers are called to actively access and apply these blessings now, impacting their lives and the lives of others around them.
- **Contrast Between Spiritual and Material Blessings:** While material blessings address physical needs, spiritual blessings address eternal and spiritual needs, providing believers with the tools needed for spiritual warfare, kingdom advancement, and personal sanctification.
- **Role of Faith in Accessing Blessings:** Accessing spiritual blessings requires faith and spiritual awareness. Believers must understand their spiritual bank of resources and learn to draw from it through faith, much like accessing funds in a bank account.
- **Transformation Through Spiritual Inheritance:** By embracing their spiritual inheritance, believers undergo a transformation that shifts their identity to align with their heavenly status. This identity shift is crucial for living out the fullness of life that God intends for each believer.

Conclusion

Spiritual blessings are crucial for a believer's life, providing not only the authority and power to operate in the spiritual realm but also influencing their everyday lives. This chapter calls believers to a deeper understanding and engagement with the spiritual resources available in Christ, encouraging them to live as empowered, effective agents of God's kingdom. By recognizing and utilizing these blessings, believers can fulfill their divine destinies and bring glory to God through a life richly endowed with His grace and power.

CHAPTER 8
SPIRITUALLY ASCENDING

Bible Verse

Luke 4:18 19 (KJV)   "The Spirit of the Lord is upon me, because he hath anointed me to preach the gospel to the poor; he hath sent me to heal the brokenhearted, to preach deliverance to the captives, and recovering of sight to the blind, to set at liberty them that are bruised, To preach the acceptable year of the Lord."

Introduction

This chapter explores how Jesus exemplified living in a spiritual dimension while on Earth, providing a model for believers to emulate. It emphasizes the concept of spiritual ascension as a daily, accessible reality rather than a rare supernatural event.

Word of Wisdom

"He did what he saw the Father doing, and He said what He heard the Fa-

ther say" – This encapsulates the essence of living a spiritually ascended life. Isaac Pitre

Main Theme

Spiritual ascension involves operating in a heavenly dimension through daily life on Earth, enabled by the Holy Spirit, as demonstrated by Jesus and practiced by His disciples.

Key Points

• Jesus lived an "ascended life" before His physical ascension, demonstrating heavenly authority on Earth.

• Spiritual ascension is not limited to supernatural experiences but is accessible in everyday Christian living.

• Jesus and the disciples performed miracles as evidence of their heavenly mandate, achievable by all believers.

• True spiritual ascension involves emulating Jesus' example of dependency on the Holy Spirit.

• Ascension allows believers to operate above natural limitations, influencing both spiritual and earthly realms.

• The practices of Jesus and His disciples offer a blueprint for spiritual authority and kingdom living.

Key Themes

- **Empowerment by the Holy Spirit:** The Holy Spirit plays a crucial role in spiritual ascension, enabling believers to exceed natural capabilities and operate with divine authority, as Jesus did.
- **Practical Daily Ascension:** Spiritual ascension is a daily reality, not confined to extraordinary moments; it involves living out heavenly principles and authority in everyday situations and challenges.
- **Template of Jesus' Life:** Jesus' life serves as a template for spiritual ascension, showing that it involves both proclaiming and demonstrating the kingdom of God through tangible acts and spiritual authority.
- **Transformation Through Renewed Mind:** Ascending spiritually requires a transformation of the mind to align with divine perspectives, emphasizing the necessity of thinking and acting from a position of spiritual reality.
- **Impact of Ascended Living:** Living an ascended life impacts the earthly realm by bringing spiritual solutions and breakthroughs to worldly problems, manifesting the kingdom of God visibly and effectively.

Conclusion

Spiritual ascension is about transcending earthly limitations through the power of the Holy Spirit, as demonstrated by Jesus. This chapter encourages believers to actively engage in spiritual ascension, utilizing the divine authority and insights bestowed upon them to influence both spiritual and physical realms. By adopting Jesus' approach to daily living, believers can bring heavenly solutions to earthly challenges, fulfilling their divine mandate to establish God's kingdom on Earth.

CHAPTER 9

I GO TO PREPARE A PLACE FOR YOU

Bible Verse

John 14:2 (KJV) - "In my Father's house are many mansions: if it were not so, I would have told you. I go to prepare a place for you."

Introduction

This chapter reinterprets Jesus' promise of preparing a place for believers, emphasizing the immediate and earthly implications of ascension and its empowering effect on believers' lives today, rather than focusing solely on the heavenly afterlife.

Word of Wisdom

"Jesus is getting ready to transition the disciples into apostles as the foundation of a brand-new church that He is

about to birth after the resurrection."
Isaac Pitre

Main Theme

The chapter illuminates how Jesus' teachings about going to the Father and preparing a place are linked to enabling believers to perform greater works through the Holy Spirit, reflecting a shift from physical presence to spiritual empowerment.

Key Points

• Jesus' preparation of a place is linked to spiritual empowerment, not just a promise of heavenly residence.

• The disciples' ability to perform greater works is tied to Jesus' ascension and the subsequent descent of the Holy Spirit.

• Jesus' physical departure was necessary for the spiritual empowerment of the Church.

• Ascension teachings emphasize a living, dynamic faith active in the world today.

• Believers are called to access and utilize the authority given through Christ's ascension.

• Jesus assures believers of continuous communion with Him and the Father through the Holy Spirit.

Key Themes

- **Empowerment through Ascension:** Jesus' ascension isn't just about His departure to heaven but is fundamentally about empowering believers on earth with the Holy Spirit, enabling them to extend His work beyond what was seen during His physical presence.
- **Immediate Access to Divine Presence:** Through the ascension, believers gain immediate and continuous access to the Father through Jesus, empowering them to live out their heavenly mandate on earth effectively and dynamically.
- **Transformation of Understanding:** The chapter calls for a transformation in understanding the scriptures from a purely future heavenly promise to a present, powerful, and practical reality of living in an ascended state with Christ.
- **Living in the 'Father's House':** The concept of living in the 'Father's House' is redefined from a physical dwelling place in heaven to a spiritual state of being that believers enter into here and now, enabling a life of miraculous works and divine presence.
- **Spiritual Reality of the Believer's Life:** The spiritual reality promised through ascension is a current, active, and dynamic engagement with the world, demonstrating the kingdom of God through empowered believers.

Conclusion

This chapter reframes the traditional understanding of Jesus' promise to prepare a place for believers, emphasizing the present and active role of the Holy Spirit in empowering believers for greater works. It calls believers to embrace their role in the Father's house here and now, equipped and empowered by the Holy Spirit to fulfill the mission and ministry of Jesus on earth.

CHAPTER 10

ANGELS ASCENDING AND DESCENDING

Bible Verse

Hebrews 1:14 (KJV)   "Are they not all ministering spirits, sent forth to minister for them who shall be heirs of salvation?"

Introduction

This chapter explores the profound spiritual authority given to the Church to govern the spiritual realm, emphasizing the dynamic interaction between believers and angels as depicted in biblical narratives and the empowering implications for daily Christian living.

Word of Wisdom

"Angels are sent to minister or serve, those of us who are heirs of salvation."
Isaac Pitre

Main Theme

The Church's role in the spiritual realm extends beyond earthly boundaries, involving active engagement with angels who minister according to God's will and the believer's authority in Christ.

Key Points

• Believers hold supremacy in the spiritual world, governing with authority granted by Jesus' ascension.

• Angels, previously unseen participants in God's plan, now serve the heirs of salvation.

• Our spiritual position is reinforced by scriptural examples where angelic beings interact with humans.

• Jesus' life demonstrates how believers can live under an open heaven with angels actively participating.

• The Church is tasked with continuing Jesus' ministry on earth, utilizing angelic assistance for spiritual and earthly governance.

Key Themes

• **Biblical Foundation of Angelic Interaction:** The Scriptures reveal that angels are deeply involved in the unfolding of God's salvation plan, a mystery that even angels desired to look into, demonstrating the intertwined destinies of humanity and the angelic host.

- **Strategic Role of Angels in Christian Doctrine:** Angels are not just observers but active participants in the kingdom of God, tasked with assisting believers in their earthly journey and spiritual battles, as seen in the dynamic visions of Jacob and Jesus' teachings.
- **Living under an Open Heaven:** Believers are invited to live a life characterized by direct access to spiritual resources, where angelic beings ascend and descend, facilitating God's work on earth as they did in the life of Jesus.
- **Empowered by Ascension:** The ascension of Jesus marks a transition of authority to believers, who now engage in spiritual warfare and governance with angels as their ministers, reinforcing the Church's heavenly mandate on earth.
- **Practical Implications for Daily Living:** Understanding our role in relation to angels encourages believers to exercise their spiritual authority confidently, knowing that their commands in Christ influence spiritual activities and real-world outcomes.

Conclusion

"Angels Ascending and Descending" affirms the Church's elevated role in the spiritual hierarchy, endowed with the authority to command angelic forces in the fulfillment of God's purposes. This chapter calls believers to embrace their identity as rulers in the spiritual realm, actively engaging with angelic beings to bring about God's will on earth as it is in heaven. Through this empowered understanding, believers are encouraged to live out their faith with the assurance that the heavenly realm responds to their God-given authority.

CHAPTER 11

THE FINISHED WORK

Bible Verse

Ephesians 1:22 (KJV)   "And hath put all things
under his feet, and gave him to be the head over all
things to the church."

Introduction

This chapter delves into the profound
reality that believers have entered into the
completed work of Christ, emphasizing
the authority and victory that have been secured
through His resurrection and ascension.

Word of Wisdom

"Through Christ, your foot is on the
enemy's back forever." Isaac Pitre

Main Theme

The central theme explores the "finished work" of Christ, focusing on the believer's position of authority over spiritual adversaries, established by Christ's ultimate sacrifice and ongoing intercession.

Key Points

• Christ's work of redemption is complete, with all enemies placed under His authority.

• Believers are seated with Christ, sharing in His authority over spiritual realms.

• The Church is called to enforce Christ's victory actively.

• Our victory and authority in Christ are permanent and irrevocable.

• Spiritual warfare is conducted from the position of victory already won.

• The promises of God are realized and accessed through Christ.

Key Themes

• **Prophetic Foundations and Fulfillment:** Biblical prophecies such as Psalm 110 and their fulfillment in the New Testament underscore the Messiah's seated authority and the believer's participation in this divine order, establishing a framework for understanding our spiritual jurisdiction.

- **Enforcing Christ's Victory:** As believers seated in heavenly places, our role extends beyond passive observance to active enforcement of the victory Christ achieved, engaging in spiritual warfare with the authority He has delegated to us.
- **Understanding Our Spiritual Position:** It's essential for believers to grasp their elevated position alongside Christ to effectively exercise the 'footstool ministry,' where we maintain dominion over spiritual adversaries as part of our inherited authority.
- **The Reality of the Finished Work:** The chapter calls for a renewed mindset among believers to align with the reality of Christ's finished work, encouraging us to speak and act from this position of victory and authority.
- **Living in the Victory of Christ:** Emphasizing the permanence of our victory in Christ, the chapter encourages believers to operate from a standpoint of triumph in all spiritual and earthly engagements, leveraging the 'finished work' in daily life and ministry.

Conclusion

"The Finished Work" profoundly articulates that believers are not just recipients but active participants in Christ's victory. This chapter reorients the believer's understanding and practical living to align with the truths of Christ's complete work on the cross, urging a life that consistently reflects and enforces this divine victory and authority. This understanding is crucial for walking in the fullness of the power and rights bestowed upon us through Christ's ascension, impacting how we engage with the world and the spiritual realm.

CHAPTER 12

UNMOVABLE SEAT

Bible Verse

Ephesians 1:18 (KJV) - "The eyes of your understanding being enlightened; that ye may know what is the hope of his calling, and what the riches of the glory of his inheritance in the saints."

Introduction

This chapter emphasizes the permanence and significance of the believer's spiritual position in Christ, secured through His intercession and the believer's acceptance into heavenly places.

Word of Wisdom

"Jesus ever lives in this position to keep me at peace with God by giving me His position. Grace is so amazing!" Isaac Pitre

Main Theme

The core theme revolves around the secure and unshakable position of believers, seated with Christ in heavenly places, far above all spiritual adversaries.

Key Points

• Believers are seated with Christ in an unchangeable position of authority.

• Jesus continuously intercedes for us, ensuring our position is secure.

• Our spiritual authority is rooted in Christ's intercessory role at God's right hand.

• We are called to enforce this authority over principalities and powers.

• The victory and authority we hold are part of Christ's finished work.

• Understanding our seated position is crucial for exercising spiritual dominion.

Key Themes

- **Intercession and Permanence:** Jesus' ongoing intercession for believers is not just a temporary role but a permanent assurance that maintains our place in God's presence, reinforcing our unmovable seat beside Him.

- **Revelation of Our Position:** It's vital for believers to understand the depth of their invitation to sit with Christ, recognizing the authority and expectations that accompany this spiritual positioning.
- **The Unchanging Nature of Our Seat:** The chapter stresses that our seat alongside Christ is permanent and immune to changes, regardless of worldly or spiritual challenges, highlighting the eternal stability provided by Christ's victory.
- **Authority Over Spiritual Adversaries:** Believers are equipped to exercise dominion over spiritual enemies, not through physical might but through the spiritual authority granted by our ascension with Christ.
- **Living from a Place of Victory:** The practical implications of understanding our seated position involve actively enforcing the victory Christ secured, which is critical for overcoming spiritual challenges and advancing God's kingdom.

Conclusion

"Unmovable Seat" underlines the believer's firm and secured position in Christ, transcending earthly and spiritual fluctuations. It calls for a deepened awareness and utilization of this spiritual stature to live victoriously and fulfill God's purposes on earth. The chapter urges believers to embrace and operate from this position of authority, continually reinforced by Christ's eternal intercession, ensuring that we remain steadfast and

unmovable in our spiritual and earthly
engagements.

CHAPTER 13

ASCENSION LIVING

Bible Verse

John 17:1 6 (KJV) "These words spake Jesus, and lifted up his eyes to heaven, and said, Father, the hour is come; glorify thy Son, that thy Son also may glorify thee."

Introduction

This chapter explores the life of Jesus as a model for living an ascended life on earth, emphasizing the potential for believers to live in a similar spiritual stature due to Christ's work.

Word of Wisdom

"Jesus could have waited until we got to Heaven to sit us down, but He did it while we were still on earth, so we could

reveal to humanity and principalities the superiority of a life in Christ." Isaac Pitre

Main Theme

Ascension Living delineates how Jesus exemplified a heavenly life on earth to demonstrate what believers can achieve through His finished work, emphasizing that the ascended life is both a present reality and a future promise.

Key Points

• Jesus' earthly life was a preview of the ascended life believers can lead.

• Christ's earthly actions were from an ascended position of authority.

• Jesus performed his ministry as a man filled with divine glory.

• Our ascension with Christ allows us to live an abundant life now.

• Believers are called to manifest the quality of life Jesus demonstrated.

• The ascended life affects our everyday behavior and relationships.

Key Themes

- **Divine Authority in Human Experience:** Though Jesus operated on earth within human limitations, He accessed divine authority, demonstrating that believers too are empowered to live from a position of heavenly authority.
- **Transformation Through Ascension:** Understanding Jesus' ascended life helps believers grasp the depth of transformation available to them, enabling a life that continually reflects divine nature and authority.
- **Current and Future Realities of Ascension:** The ascended life is not just about future heavenly promises but involves living out a superior quality of life here and now, characterized by divine peace, authority, and purpose.
- **Practical Implications of Ascension:** The teachings of Jesus about the blessed life reveal that ascension living impacts practical daily living, urging believers to adopt attitudes of love, peace, and joy.
- **Evangelistic Impact of Ascension Living:** By living out the ascended life, believers can dramatically influence their surroundings, showcasing the transformative power of the gospel in tangible ways.

Conclusion

Ascension Living invites believers to engage deeply with the reality of their heavenly position alongside Christ. It challenges readers to live out their divine inheritance daily, influencing their environments through the superior life quality that comes from being seated with Christ in heavenly places. The chapter underscores that embracing and manifesting this ascended life is key to fulfilling Christ's mission on earth, offering a compelling witness to the transformative power of the gospel.

CHAPTER 14

ASCENSION POWER

Bible Verse

Mark 16:15-20 (KJV) - "And he said unto them, Go ye into all the world, and preach the gospel to every creature. He that believeth and is baptized shall be saved; but he that believeth not shall be damned."

Introduction

This chapter explores the authority and power believers hold through Christ's ascension, emphasizing the active engagement and supernatural abilities that follow those who believe and operate in this truth.

Word of Wisdom

"We should all be preaching to the believer what Jesus, Paul, Peter, James, and John preached. We don't need anything else." Isaac Pitre

Main Theme

Ascension Power underscores the transformative potential for believers to execute works greater than those Jesus performed, rooted in the elevated position granted through His ascension.

Key Points

• Believers are granted authority to perform miracles and spiritual acts as Christ did.

• Our spiritual position is established in heavenly places, above all adversarial powers.

• The fivefold ministry is crucial for equipping the Church to operate in ascension power.

• Jesus's ministry and the empowerment of the Holy Spirit are models for our potential.

• Believers are called to manifest God's power on Earth through spiritual gifts.

• Understanding and operating in these gifts are central to fulfilling our divine mandate.

Key Themes

• **Empowerment Through Ascension:** The power and authority granted through ascension equip believers to perform supernatural acts, mirroring Jesus's earthly ministry. This includes healing, exorcism, and speaking in new tongues, showcasing the continuation of Jesus's work through His followers.

- **Role of the Fivefold Ministry:** The apostle, prophet, evangelist, pastor, and teacher are tasked with aligning the Church's understanding and operation in the power of ascension. Proper teaching and equipping in this area are essential for the Church to realize its full potential in Christ.

- **Importance of Spiritual Gifts:** Spiritual gifts are manifestations of the Holy Spirit that empower believers to operate beyond natural capabilities. These gifts are not just for building the Church but also for demonstrating God's kingdom on Earth.

- **Necessity of Faith and Understanding:** Believers must cultivate a robust faith and deep understanding of their spiritual authority to effectively wield the power available to them in Christ. This includes overcoming fear and doubt that hinder the activation of these spiritual gifts.

- **Integration of Ascension Truths in Ministry:** The ascension and seating of Christ are fundamental doctrines that should permeate the teachings and operational ethos of modern Christian ministry. Emphasizing these truths can transform the spiritual dynamics of believers' lives and their impact on the world.

Conclusion

Ascension Power calls believers to a higher level of spiritual operation, where understanding and actively engaging in the ascended life Christ has provided leads to tangible manifestations of divine power. By embracing our seated position with Christ in heavenly places, believers can transcend normal human limits and bring about supernatural change in the world, effectively continuing the ministry of Jesus on Earth. This power is not just a theological concept but a practical reality meant to be experienced and demonstrated daily.

CHAPTER 15

KINGDOM ESTABLISHMENT

Bible Verse

Ephesians 1:9-10 (KJV) - "Having made known unto us the mystery of his will, according to his good pleasure which he hath purposed in himself: That in the dispensation of the fulness of times he might gather together in one all things in Christ, both which are in heaven, and which are on earth; even in him."

Introduction

This chapter delves into the profound implications of Christ's ascension, highlighting the authority bestowed upon believers to bring all elements under the dominion of Jesus, thus fulfilling God's ultimate plan for unity through Christ.

Word of Wisdom

"Because Jesus is the exalted One, you

and I are exalted ones and must learn to live from this exalted state." Isaac Pitre

Main Theme

The main theme centers on the spiritual authority and responsibility of believers to govern and reign with Christ, emphasizing the role of the Church in establishing God's kingdom on Earth as it is in Heaven.

Key Points

• Jesus's ascension was designed to unify all things under His governance.

• Believers are called to live from an exalted, heavenly seated position.

• The concept of Reignology emphasizes our role as rulers with Christ.

• Our spiritual authority is meant to be actively exercised against spiritual opposition.

• Teaching and embracing this reign is crucial for the Church's victory.

• Our position in Christ empowers us to manifest the kingdom of God on Earth.

Key Themes

• **Spiritual Dominion and Authority:** As believers seated with Christ in heavenly places, we possess the authority to influence both spiritual and earthly realms. This dominion is not just about reigning in a future afterlife but actively engaging in spiritual governance now, affecting change and asserting God's rule across all creation.

- **Reignology as Christian Practice:** Reignology, or the theology of reigning with Christ, transforms our understanding of spiritual authority, encouraging believers to adopt a mindset of kingship. This perspective involves seeing ourselves as active participants in enforcing Christ's victory over demonic forces and earthly challenges.

- **Educational Imperative in Church Doctrine:** It is vital for church leaders to instruct congregations about their heavenly positions and the power that comes with it. Understanding our place with Christ helps believers to operate from a stance of victory rather than defeat.

- **The Practical Outworking of Ascension:** The daily life of a believer should reflect the ascension power that Christ has conferred upon us. This means living out our heavenly mandate here on Earth by exercising authority over spiritual wickedness and manifesting the qualities of the kingdom in all areas of life.

- **Unification Under Christ's Authority:** The ultimate goal of Christ's exaltation is the unification of all things under His authority. Believers are called to actively participate in this process, ensuring that

Christ's sovereignty is acknowledged in the spiritual and physical realms.

Conclusion

Kingdom Establishment articulates the believer's role in God's grand design, emphasizing that the ascension of Christ is a call to action for every Christian to live out a powerful, kingdom-oriented life. This chapter encourages readers to embrace their identity as rulers with Christ, using their God-given authority to bring about God's will on Earth, thus playing an integral part in the unfolding of divine prophecy and the establishment of eternal justice and peace.

CHAPTER 16

RELEASING THE HEAVENS OVER YOUR LIFE

Bible Verse

Ephesians 2:5 7 (KJV) - "Even when we were dead in sins, hath quickened us together with Christ, (by grace ye are saved;) And hath raised us up together, and made us sit together in heavenly places in Christ Jesus: That in the ages to come he might shew the exceeding riches of his grace in his kindness toward us through Christ Jesus."

Introduction

This chapter explores the concept of living in the "Ascension Dimension," emphasizing the believer's dual existence in both earthly and heavenly realms, and how to effectively harness heavenly authority to influence earthly circumstances.

Word of Wisdom

"Praying and decreeing are vital

parts of ascension living because every-thing done in Christ has been done!"
Isaac Pitre

Main Theme

The primary focus of this chapter is on the believers' elevated position with Christ in heavenly places and the practical implications of this spiritual status in their daily lives and prayer practices.

Key Points

• We are raised with Christ and seated in heavenly places.

• Our spiritual position allows us to influence earthly conditions.

• Prayer is the mechanism through which we release heavenly authority on earth.

• Persistence in prayer reflects a posture of faith and expectation.

• Understanding our authority is key to exercising it effectively.

• Decreeing God's will on earth is an act of dominion and alignment with His purposes.

Key Themes

• **Heavenly Positioning and Earthly Impact:** Being seated in heavenly places positions us to exert influence over earthly matters through divine authority. This spiritual status is not just theoretical but has real-world implications that allow believers to shape their environments according to God's will.

- **Prayer as a Release of Divine Authority:** Prayer is not merely a request for help but a declaration of God's will on earth as it is in heaven. It is the believer's tool to bring the resources, provisions, and powers of heaven into their earthly experiences, aligning their surroundings with God's purposes.
- **Persistence in Prayer:** Jesus' teachings on prayer underscore the importance of persistence, portraying it as a reflection of faith rather than a sign of desperation. This tenacity in prayer acknowledges God as the ultimate source and aligns our requests with His sovereign will.
- **Authority in Christ's Ascension:** The ascension of Christ is pivotal in understanding the believers' authority. It is from this position of raised and seated with Christ that believers derive the right and power to command earthly circumstances.
- **Integrating Kingdom Principles in Daily Life:** The chapter emphasizes the importance of abiding in Christ and His words to unlock the promises and powers available to believers. It is crucial for believers to maintain their spiritual position and integrity to fully exercise their heavenly mandates.

Conclusion

"Releasing the Heavens Over Your Life" encourages believers to live from a place of divine authority, rooted in Christ's ascension. By understanding and applying the principles of heavenly positioning and authoritative prayer, believers can manifest God's kingdom on earth, transforming their lives and their environments through the power vested in them by Christ. This chapter calls for a deepened faith and a committed application of spiritual truths to realize the full potential of our elevated position with Jesus.

CHAPTER 17

YOU HAVE THE ADVANTAGE

Bible Verse

John 16:7 (KJV) - "Nevertheless I tell you the truth; It is expedient for you that I go away: for if I go not away, the Comforter will not come unto you; but if I depart, I will send him unto you."

Introduction

This chapter underscores the profound significance of the Holy Spirit's role in believers' lives, explaining that the Ascension of Jesus was necessary for the Spirit's arrival, which empowers believers to live in the Ascension Dimension.

Word of Wisdom

"The mind of God cannot be known, it must be revealed by the Spirit, because it

is the Spirit who searches all the deep things of God." Isaac Pitre

Main Theme

The main theme of this chapter is the transformative power of the Holy Spirit in enabling believers to access divine wisdom and live in a supernatural dimension, transcending natural limitations.

Key Points

• The Ascension was essential for the Holy Spirit's descent.

• The Holy Spirit allows believers to access God's wisdom.

• Spiritual insights are revealed, not learned.

• Speaking in tongues is a direct communication with God.

• Believers have a significant advantage over spiritual adversaries.

• The Spirit teaches and guides in all truths.

Key Themes

• **Role of the Holy Spirit in the Ascension Dimension:** The Holy Spirit serves as a bridge connecting believers to the divine, enabling them to live a life that transcends the natural through direct communication and insight from God. This divine connector empowers believers to access and apply heavenly wisdom to earthly challenges.

- **Advantage of Spiritual Insight:** With the Holy Spirit, believers gain a competitive spiritual advantage, capable of accessing hidden wisdom and operating with a level of divine foresight that is inaccessible to those not in tune with the Spirit. This enables believers to navigate life with God-guided precision and authority.

- **Practicality of Spiritual Living:** The chapter emphasizes the practical aspects of spiritual living, encouraging believers to engage in daily practices that foster a vibrant relationship with the Holy Spirit. These practices include praying in tongues, which enhances spiritual sensitivity and communication with God.

- **Combatting Spiritual Ignorance:** By explaining the function and necessity of the Holy Spirit, the author aims to counteract the enemy's efforts to diminish the Spirit's role in the church, highlighting the indispensable need for believers to embrace the fullness of the Spirit's power and ministry.

- **Integration of the Spiritual into the Daily:** The Spirit filled life is portrayed not as a series of sporadic supernatural events but as a continuous living in the supernatural, where everyday actions and decisions are influenced by divine guidance and the inherent authority given through the Ascension.

Conclusion

"You Have the Advantage" inspires believers to embrace their elevated life in the Spirit, encouraging a deep, ongoing engagement with the Holy Spirit as essential for living out the fullness of their divine inheritance. This chapter challenges believers to not only acknowledge their spiritual authority but to actively engage with the Holy Spirit in manifesting God's kingdom on earth, thereby living out the true potential of their ascension with Christ.